Investing

The World's Biggest Untapped Opportunity: A Value
Investor's Guide

*(A Three-step Plan For Building Recession-resilient
Wealth)*

Broderick Santana

TABLE OF CONTENT

How To Start Investing In Stocks

Stock market trading used to be a kind of investing reserved for the wealthy and those with the necessary financial connections. However, this has changed due to the explosive expansion of online trading, and now anyone with money may participate in the buying and selling of stocks.

The acquisition of the required information and comprehension of the proper stock market terms is the most fundamental necessity for beginners to engage in stock trading. The truth is that your chances of succeeding in producing money increase with your level of financial knowledge. It is significant to highlight that since stock trading depends on the growth and fall of share values, it differs significantly from other forms of earning money. Before engaging in this type of trade, you should gather the appropriate information to avoid losing your money too soon. In general, equities outperform assets like gold, treasury bills, and bonds.

Especially if you've never traded stocks before, the procedure can be rather scary. Starting is easier than you might think if you have the appropriate information. The ability to start trading on the stock market with as little as $500 in money is one benefit. You need to first ask yourself some important questions that will define your experience in stock trading before you can grasp what is needed to get started. Several of these queries include:

• Why are you making this investment? What percentage of the time will you be dedicating to it? You need to be clear about your trade execution strategy. If you are employed, you must decide when and how frequently you will conduct research each day or each week. In answering this question, you must also decide whether you want to become a short-term or long-term investor and how long you intend to stay in the stock market. This will assist you in selecting the best trading approach to leverage your gains. For instance, depending on your needs and availability, you will be able to decide if you need to adopt day trading, swing trading, or long-term trading.

Are you a risk-taker? There are numerous hazards while trading stocks.

Generally speaking, higher gains come with increased risk. Are you able to invest in high-risk investments that have a decent chance of success? Can you sustain the losses associated with the trade? Will you continue trading if you end up losing all of your investment money? You are the best candidate for the stock market if your response to these questions is yes. If you are someone who avoids taking chances, you might want to think about alternative equities investments like index funds, which carry lower risk.

What percentage of your time do you plan to devote to stock trading?

If you have a limited amount of time, you should invest in stocks rather than funds. The majority of your time is not needed to invest in funds. This is because the fund management will choose the appropriate stocks for you to invest in. Since you have to evaluate markets and project earnings, stocks are frequently more time-consuming.

Starting Points: Steps

You can begin investing in the stock market as a beginner by following the straightforward steps listed below.

1. Decide on your investment strategy.

You can purchase shares using a variety of methods. Your method of choice will rely on a variety of variables. You have two options: you can trade on your own, or you may hire a broker to do it for you. Since the broker handles almost everything, including making stock orders, negotiating the best prices, and delivering financial advice, most beginners choose the second option.

Investment funds

You might start off better off investing in mutual funds rather than straight equities. This is due to the fact that funds are managed by experts who want to relieve you of the responsibility of selecting the best equities to trade with. All you have to do to get started is decide how much money you want to invest into the fund. Since each fund covers a variety of stocks, investing in mutual funds has the benefit of relieving you of the responsibility of portfolio diversification.

Indices Funds

In comparison to mutual funds and stocks, these are simpler to trade. Mutual fund types called index funds follow financial market indices. These funds have lower operational costs than regular funds and have a wider exposure in terms of the stocks they invest in. Index funds have the benefit of remaining constant despite fluctuations in stock market prices. They are quite prevalent in both 401(k) and retirement plans.

2. Create a profile

If you don't have an account, you can never list stocks or make investments on the stock market. This could be a brokerage account or an individual investing account. A brokerage account is among the most affordable methods for purchasing stocks. You can also open an individual retirement account, or IRA, through a broker. You can open a taxable brokerage account if you don't want to use an IRA account. Consider factors including commissions and account fees, investment choices, and the kinds of tools the broker can provide when deciding which broker to work with.

You can locate a broker offline or online, just in your neighborhood. Once you've found one, you'll have to deposit some money and sign some documents in order to start an account.

Account for Individual Retirement

When it comes to long-term investing, this form of account is the finest. IRAs are typically loaded mostly from your payroll and are frequently tax-exempt. Saving money in this kind of account for many years might be very beneficial for your retirement. You can save money in an IRA for as long as you choose before deciding whether to invest it in the stock market. With this account, there is no rush to enter the market because you won't begin trading until you feel comfortable doing so.

Trading Account

The IRA and a brokerage account are almost the same thing. It cannot be used to accumulate money for upcoming ventures. The fact that some brokerage accounts have very cheap commissions and no minimum cash deposit requirement is an advantage. This form of account has the disadvantage of having a cap on the investments you can make. You only put money in the account with the intention of engaging in stock market trading.

the part brokers play

Brokers help sellers and buyers conduct efficient transactions. You should take into account a number of variables when looking for a reputable broker. A reliable broker is one who:

charges minimal brokerage costs and commissions

is trustworthy in terms of accessibility

is dependable. Someone who won't steal your money or utilize it in unscrupulous ways

gives you access to the tools you need for study. Some of these can be found online for no cost.

If you plan to become a day trader, the broker you select must be able to fulfill orders promptly because any delay could lead to significant losses. Additionally, the broker should be able to comprehend and analyze day charts, and quickly modify your orders in accordance with these readings.

Additionally, keep in mind that not all brokers are suitable for investors. Some are best suited to swing and day traders alone. If you intend to invest in stocks for the long term, you must be sure that the broker you choose can maximize your return on investment. Since the individual will be in control of your capital and your success depends on his knowledge and experience, choosing a broker carefully is crucial. Before investing your money in a broker, make sure to test out their platform. In addition to letting you place purchase orders, a decent platform will give you access to a variety of trading charts, stock quotations, and research materials.

3. Create the budget

The idea of entering stock trading without a clear plan is the riskiest aspect of it, if there is one. To start, you must first determine how much you require. You will pay this sum in order to buy your stocks. The value of the shares you choose is what matters most. Share prices can range from a few pennies to several thousands of dollars. If you have a small amount of money, exchange-traded funds are an option because they require less money to get started.

Consider your whole financial situation as you create a budget. Make sure that the activities you desire to engage in can be sustained in your current employment. In order to do this, you must evaluate your income, expenses, and any outstanding debts. You must first determine whether your income is reliable enough to support your investment. If you have a lot of debt, you might want to think about paying it off before investing in stocks since you might find yourself in trouble if the value of the stock market falls. This may be particularly challenging if your debt repayment is dependent on market returns. You are encouraged to only invest money that you can afford to lose because of this. How much you should invest in the stock market depends on your household budget as well. Choose a sum that will leave you with enough money for home expenses.

After determining your needs, save some money as a backup in case things don't work out as you had hoped. A cash reserve is what is referred to as this. It is advised that you set aside enough money to cover your expenses for at least three months. You require the cash reserve for two reasons. First, it will help you if you face financial difficulty, particularly if your investment fails. The reserve also gives you peace of mind in case you lose your other source of income.

4. Invest

When investing in stocks, you can use a variety of tactics. While some are simpler and easier to understand, others are more complex. Most expert investors who are adept at stock market techniques use these. Look into the stocks or funds you wish to invest your time and money in, then choose one that has more rewards and less dangers.

Choose businesses with growth potential because they will provide you with profitable investments.

Do not invest all of your funds in the shares once you have chosen the type to buy. Instead, steadily enter the market and increase your investment levels over time. This will help you out much if the market doesn't behave as you had anticipated. In the past, some traders have made significant investments on the market, and as soon as they did, the prices began to fall. They ended up incurring substantial financial losses. It is crucial that you take your time because of this. As you keep an eye on the market and discover new strategies, trade in some items. Never forget to set aside some time each week to evaluate your prior performance. You can use this to find out where you need to improve.

The dollar cost averaging method, which reduces stock price swings, is not used when trading individual stocks. This implies that you must manually develop such a method by calculating the appropriate investment amount for each time that shares are listed on the stock market.

You can gradually incorporate individual stocks into your investment strategy once you have mastered trading in funds and other financial instruments. It is suggested that you start by allocating just a modest portion of your wealth to stock investments. Most newcomers begin with no more than 10% of their total money. Make sure not to take more than one position in a single stock while you do this. Take small holdings in the stock of your choice and keep investing in it until you have mastered trading many stock types.

Managing Your Money

There is a minimum amount of capital required for any trading method that you employ. You must have at least $25,000 in your stock account, for instance, if you choose to day trade on a US stock exchange. Swing trading offers an advantage over other methods in that there are no constraints on the minimum capital needed. Despite this, you still need at least $10,000 to make trading in other kinds of stock possible. Long-term investing methods don't need a lot of capital to be invested in them. Due to the longer duration of the deal, these strategies also charge lower charges.

So, as soon as you have enough money, you can start investing in stocks. By executing one trade at a time rather than numerous deals simultaneously when trading, you can lower the fee costs. For instance, you may save money for a month and then make one sizable purchase rather than buying 100 shares every week. However, this only applies when there are high commission rates and low transaction values. It doesn't matter if you make recurring investments for big stock purchases because the commissions won't go down very significantly.

5. Ensure Stock Portfolio Diversity

When you first begin investing, be careful not to focus solely on one kind of stock. For instance, you shouldn't invest all of your money in one sector, such as biotechnology stocks. Despite the potential for huge returns, this turns out to be excessively hazardous in the event that the value of such shares declines quickly. Spreading your money throughout a variety of industries, such as real estate, commodities, consumer products, or insurance, is a good idea. To be on the safe side, you can also invest some money in bonds and mutual funds.

You can think about investing a larger portion of your initial investment in mutual funds. This increases the variety of your stock market and gives you exposure abroad. When compared to when you limit yourself to just one class of stocks, a diverse portfolio offers you a more consistent revenue stream.

For instance, if you wish to invest in individual stocks, you have a better chance of seeing significant returns if your portfolio includes at least 12 different equities from solid companies. But in this situation, you'll need to be aware of each stock's hazards as well as the firm that backs it. Make sure to distribute your wealth over several stock sectors if you don't wish to invest in bonds or funds. Depending on how the market is doing at the time, mix small, medium, and large cap stocks.

As you continue to trade and gain experience, keep refining your stock picks once you've established your equity portfolio. Sell some of the stocks with lower priority and replace them on a regular basis with equities with a better market value. By include some companies and funds in the industries you want to grow your exposure to, you may also strengthen your portfolio. These additions can be used to increase returns and provide you with longer-term earnings.

Setting aside cash reserves is another aspect of diversification. You have started the process of diversification whenever you include more than one type of investment in your plan. Make sure to diversify your holdings in equities in case one doesn't perform well. For example, you might think about expanding your portfolio by including bonds, income funds, and international funds in your trading strategy. Additionally, keep an eye out for stocks with greater dividends and add them to your list of specific equities. These provide you a solid place to start because you can be certain that you will earn from each of them. It is essential to invest in income funds since they perform well in gloomy markets and have less volatility than ordinary stocks.

You must learn to balance your investments in numerous assets. There are numerous businesses online that can easily assist you with this. They give you advice on how to allocate your investment capital and how to properly diversify.

6. Amass Some Investment Information

When dealing with ETFs and mutual funds, you do not need to study anything about investing, but it is crucial that you gain the knowledge necessary for stock trading before investing in the company. You can begin investing as soon as you have collected the necessary funds when using mutual funds, index funds, or ETFs because specialists will execute the trades on your behalf. However, if you choose to trade specific equities, you will need to do additional study before making market investments.

The majority of new traders study individual equities with the time they would have spent trading collective funds and ETFs. In the future, if you're interested in trading stocks directly, you should learn as much as you can about the investment because it will affect how well you do on the market. You can get all the knowledge you require in a number of books, magazines, blogs, and audio CDs. Additionally, you can choose to join an investment forum or enroll in a program that covers stock investments in order to learn from industry leaders.

Once you have the essential knowledge, you can use it to develop an investing plan that is suitable for your needs. A sound plan enables you to take advantage of all investment opportunities while attempting to lower the associated dangers. Your business is very important when it comes to learning. Surround yourself with industry experts if you want to advance more quickly in the stock market. These folks will give you more confidence because they have already achieved success in fields that you are not particularly knowledgeable about.

Another option is to use an online broker's services until you feel comfortable enough to trade independently. Working with a broker has the advantage of giving you the chance to test out different tactics before to investing your money. The more you understand about stock investing, the better, as you'll be able to choose the finest assets with the best returns much more rapidly.

Stocks are tiny pieces of the businesses that sell them. A share is the unit of measurement for the cost of any given stock. The worth of a share corresponds to the worth of the underlying business. The perception of the company selling the stock by traders and investors affects how each stock performs on the market. Every day, stock prices are constantly changing.

Every stock exchange operates at specific hours. For instance, the New York Stock Exchange is open from 9:30 am to 4:00 pm Eastern time. This indicates that stock purchases and sales take place at this time for investors who choose to use the platform for trading. The majority of traders would have closed for the day, so even though trading continues outside of the designated hours, it could not present the best possibilities. Pre-market trading refers to trading that occurs before regular business hours. Following these hours is referred to as after-hours trading.

You must be familiar with the stock's ticker symbol before trading it. If you do not understand what this implies, you can get the correct symbol by typing the name of the firm that listed the stock on several online financial sites, such as Google France.

Always keep in mind that buying stocks is mostly done with the intention of making a profit. This implies that you should buy equities when they are cheap and sell them when they are expensive. Another option is to start by selling stocks at a profit and then try to buy them back at a loss. Short selling is a typical strategy utilized by short-term investors looking to benefit quickly from the market. In order to use such a method, you must first comprehend how the bid/ask spread functions since it controls how stock prices fluctuate. Additionally, you must be able to decipher stock quotes and stock charts, which aid investors in determining the direction of the market.

Prices of stocks

As you begin trading stocks, it's important to comprehend how market performance is affected by price fluctuations. Sometimes these pricing changes take place regardless of how well the underlying business is doing.

As was already mentioned, supply and demand is a major factor in the fluctuation of stock prices. This implies that a stock's price will increase automatically if it is in strong demand for some underlying reason. Stock prices will decrease if there is a decrease in demand for the stock as a result of investors choosing not to buy the stock due to the high pricing. This keeps happening until it turns into a cycle that keeps beginning. As a trader, it is your responsibility to research and comprehend these cycles in order to determine how you might profit from them. Levels of supply and demand provide insight into market behavior for new traders and investors.

Demand and supply zones may be seen on each trade chart, and these areas determine the profit margins. Any time the stock prices move into one of these areas, the market is shifting. The majority of investors buy or sell their stocks at this point. Nevertheless, depending on the original bid price for the stocks, they can gain money or lose money.

The best time to buy stocks

It's a terrific idea to buy and sell shares on the stock market. When you have sufficient knowledge of the market and how it functions, you should begin trading. It becomes simple for you to succeed in the stock market if you have the appropriate knowledge. It's conceivable that you will suffer significant stock market losses if you don't have enough knowledge about investing. Make sure to weigh the dangers involved before making any investments. Before investing your money in any stocks or shares, you must conduct thorough research on them.

Additionally, you need to be familiar with every kind of stock that may be traded in on the stock market. Additionally, you need to comprehend how each style works and how it will perform in the market. You might ask some specialists for advice if you're unsure of what to invest in. You can use these to choose the appropriate stock for your investment strategy. You can give what the experts advise a try if it makes sense to you. However, you must take care to avoid seeking advice from unskilled people who have only found success on the site by accident. Such individuals could deceive you into investing your money in unsuccessful stocks.

As you work toward realizing your investment aspirations, be sure to set and adhere to targets. The next stage is to lay out the steps that will get you significant profits. You must take your time and thoroughly research any stock market you intend to trade on in order to comprehend and adhere to the market's regulations. Steer clear of shares of companies that aren't doing well right now. Spend some time developing your profession in investments. Especially if you invest with a long-term goal in mind, you might eventually begin to get a consistent income from your investment. Before investing your money in the market, learn a few tips by using a demo or practice account.

Choosing A Broker And Carrying Out Your Investment Plans

It's time to start carrying out your plans after you've done some research and selected a few stocks to invest in in order to receive dividend income. Finding the ideal broker will be the initial step in doing so. Finding the ideal broker depends, in part, on your particular preferences. These days, the majority of brokers provide quite comparable services, so the decision may even come down to your preferred user interface. Choosing between trading on a desktop computer and a mobile device, such as a phone or tablet, is one thing to think about.

The commission fees levied by the broker are another issue that may be categorized as classic. A commission is a charge made by the broker in exchange for carrying out trades on your behalf. In the case of dividend investors, who

This is less of a problem than it is for other types of investors to be trading quite regularly. Day traders, for instance, may be making numerous transactions throughout the day and will thus be highly concerned with concerns like commissions, which can significantly reduce their profits if they are making a lot of deals.

You should start putting your investment ideas into action as soon as you are set up with a broker. You're going to have to follow through with this on a regular basis. Everyone will have their own schedule, which will be influenced in part by how you make money and when you have money to invest. But the most crucial part of this is making sure you invest frequently.

Selecting the Best Brokerage

The brokerage market has grown somewhat at this stage. So, finding brokers who have a mobile app, for example, is probably not going to be a problem for you. Second, having access to a complete set of tools that enables you to perform chart analysis is probably not going to be a concern for you because dividend investing is not an hourly or minutely activity like trading is.

Cost and convenience of usage are likely to be the main deciding factors. Nowadays, a small number of brokerages offer zero commission trading, however the majority still charge a cost to execute deals. Who could disagree with something that is free? Robinhood is one example of a brokerage with no commissions. It is a very young brokerage with an incredibly user-friendly mobile app layout. Its investing tools are also available online. The kind of analysis tools that you might find on certain trading sites that are partly designed for day traders and the like are absent from Robinhood, but as we've already said, dividend investors don't need those types of tools.

A concern for some dividend investors may be the company's stability. Many older brokerages are still operating today and are doing extremely well. Charles Schwab and Fidelity Investments are two of them. You might be willing to pay the modest commission costs to pass your investments through these brokers because these are reputable and reliable organizations. Depending on the sort of plan you choose, they might also have assistance, including financial counseling, which may or may not be useful.

TD Ameritrade and E*Trade are two other well-known brokers that have not been around as long but are nonetheless established. Early in the 1970s saw the founding of TD Ameritrade, while E*Trade was established approximately a decade earlier.

Another well-known choice that attracts many investors is Ally Invest, which is administered by Ally Bank.

They will most likely charge fees that are in the same general range as those who charge commissions. You should budget $5 to $7 every trade. Although it doesn't seem like much, it can add up. When everything is said and done, it generally won't amount to much if you are a long-term investor, but you must take it into consideration when deciding whether or not your investments are lucrative.

Robinhood is not the only broker offering no commission. An intriguing alternative is M1 Finance. In addition to having no commission, M1 Finance also enables fractional share investments. Those who are currently short on cash may want to consider this alternative; they can utilize it to at least add something to their portfolio.

Minimums for Accounts

There are account minimums for some brokers. For instance, E*Trade demands a $500 minimum balance. It's pay as you go for some. With Robinhood, you may instantly transfer money after connecting your bank account. One thing you should research before signing a contract with a broker is the account minimum. Some may have larger account minimums, but for the majority of people, a $500 threshold won't provide a significant challenge. But you do need to take into account every dollar you have to spend as part of the bigger picture. Going with a brokerage that has a $500 minimum might not be worth the wait if you are just starting out and have only $200 but are eager to start learning about stocks. In that case, you might as well just sign up for Robinhood and get begun, so at the very least you can start purchasing shares and starting your investment portfolio.

The Verdict When Selecting a Brokerage

When it comes to investing in dividends, there aren't many variations between brokerages that are worth mentioning. As we've previously stated, fancy tools like stock charts with technical indicators won't really concern you as a dividend investor. The topic of financial reports is one that people inquire about. The financial information that you will need to conduct a fundamental analysis on a potential investment target is freely available online. Therefore, a broker's presence there does not truly provide anything that you cannot receive elsewhere. For starters, they have to be simple to find on the business website. The public can see, for instance, a number of reports and filings that the SEC mandates for Apple here:

https://investor.apple.com/investor-relations/default.aspx

These kinds of formats, or at least brief descriptions, are also available on free stock market websites like Yahoo Finance. Additionally, dividend.com has a wealth of useful information that you can access. Therefore, this shouldn't be a problem.

Even though commissions are not very expensive, you can think about using a zero-commission broker because every penny counts. That way, even if they average out over time, you can make a number of trades without being concerned about rising costs.

What Takes Place If a Broker Fails?

What happens if a broker goes out of business or shuts down for other reasons is something that novice investors may wonder about. Frequently, plans can be made to merely move your account to a different broker. You might check to see if your brokerage is a member of SPIC, the Securities Investor Protection Corp. This company provides insurance for stock and bond investments up to $500,000. Cash may make up to $250,000 of this.

But keep in mind that when you purchase stock, you actually become an owner of the company; the broker is merely a middlemen. Your stock holdings in various companies shouldn't be affected if the broker eventually goes out of business.

Any money you had in your broker account that went entirely under would be a concern. The main risk is there, actually. Check to determine if the broker you chose is SPIC insured if you want to deposit substantial sums of money into your brokerage account all at once.

Just remember that the stock you possess is yours to retain, and that the brokerage has no bearing on its value, which is determined by the worth of the firm.

How to Purchase Stock

Similar to renting a movie, buying and selling stocks is simple. You simply search for the desired stock, decide how many shares you wish to buy, and submit your order. You should be aware that there are two different kinds of orders. Market orders and limit orders are what these are known as.

Most people put market orders into action. A market order is when you just click the "Buy" button after looking up a stock. As soon as it is able to, it will purchase the shares for you at the current market price. Orders on the market typically move swiftly.

You can make a limit order if you want to try and save money. Only if a buyer or seller accepts the limit price that you define will this type of order fill. Investors can attempt to purchase stocks at a discount using a limit order, assuming they can locate a seller prepared to accept the limit order price. With a limit order, you can also wait for the market to truly shift before the stock price lowers to your limit level.

Limit orders may be entered as valid till the close of business or valid until they are canceled.

Limit orders are highly helpful for traders who, for a variety of reasons, do not intend to keep stock for an extended period of time. Limit orders may not be the best use of your time and energy, though, if you're a dividend investor.

The majority of dividend investors will only place market orders.

We'll discuss crucial investment methods in the chapter after this. Purchasing your equities at regular intervals will play a part in this. Leave that irrationality to the traders; it is not the responsibility of the dividend investor to attempt to predict which direction the stock is headed. Temporary ups and downs will average out over the years you invest, and they won't have a big impact on your overall investing.

Although buying stocks more regularly is preferable, keeping to a program is more crucial. It's okay for some folks to only purchase stocks once a month. Some people may shop every two weeks when they get paid. Others might only shop once a week. Again, drawing up a plan and following it are more crucial than the time range you utilize. By developing a consistent investing routine, you'll increase your chances of having a strong portfolio that can generate the kind of income you desire by the time you retire.

Choosing Your Income Objectives

We briefly discussed how many shares you would need to own in order to reach a particular income target in the last chapter. When you begin purchasing shares, bear that in mind. If you purchase one share every month and require 4,500 shares to reach your target, doing so is probably not going to be practical for you because it would take 375 years. To achieve the desired level of income, you must therefore determine how many shares you will need and divide that number into a set of purchases that can be made on a regular basis and that can also be completed within the time frames that you have established for yourself. Therefore, if you only have 10 years to invest and you need 4,500 shares, you will need to purchase 450 shares per year. That equals roughly 38 shares every month. Depending on the stock, this may be a pricey venture. Therefore, it is preferable to begin investing early in order to achieve your objectives. As we stated in the preceding two chapters, if you are becoming older but still desire dividend income, it is likely that you will need to utilize a high growth portfolio right away. When you reach retirement age, you can begin selling shares of your high-growth equities and replacing them with dividend-paying stock. You will at least have more money to work with. Investing 65% of your money in high growth stocks and 35% in dividend stocks is a reasonable compromise because it allows you to start building a dividend portfolio while simultaneously accumulating shares of high growth companies.

Being realistic about achieving your goals is crucial. Do not worry too much about recessions or even short-term swings. Most downturns are only temporary. When a stock is experiencing a slump, you shouldn't try to estimate its annual return and then conclude that it is a bad investment. You must consider the company's overall expansion.

10,000 shares of stock is a decent target to aim for if you want to generate a solid middle-class income from dividend stocks. This is not going to be a simple accomplishment to complete for the majority of people who do not have thousands of dollars to pour into the stock market every month. Similar to the previous example, it will take a while, and you'll have to buy the lots in little quantities. For this reason, it is usually far better to begin investing when you are young. Unfortunately, money management and investment are rarely taught in our high schools or universities, and the majority of individuals lack basic financial literacy. Because our parents didn't understand finances or how to safeguard our future, many of us didn't learn anything about them as children. Many find it challenging to plan because of this. The majority of Americans do not even have the financial wherewithal to come up with $400 to cover a little emergency, as you have probably occasionally read on the news. Therefore, the majority of people do not even vaguely consider developing a long-term investing strategy that can protect their long-term future. Do not feel bad if that accurately depicts the circumstance from which you came. By reading publications like these, you are taking the initial steps toward improving your financial situation and securing your future, even though the journey there will be more challenging than it would have been if you had started earlier.

You might even think about taking on a second job if you are over 50 and find it difficult to invest large sums of money. Instead of trying to extend your working life when you might not be able to, it is preferable to work harder now, while you are still physically able to do so. After that, you can use the entire second job's earnings to launch a risky investment strategy. If you can invest

$1,000 every month for ten years, you will have invested $120,000. If you could invest $2,000 a month, you would have $240,000. With that money, you could purchase 3,692 shares of Abbvie and earn an additional $15,000 per year, which would be a wonderful supplement to social security benefits.

Everyone will have a different story because there are several scenarios and potential outcomes. However, as long as you start acting, it should be feasible to find a way out of any position you find yourself in. The intention here is not to deter consumers from buying dividend stocks since the required amount can be challenging to come up with, but rather to help them view the situation realistically.

Chapter 7: ETFs' advantages

There is more if this seems too wonderful to be true. There is no need to worry with any financial data analysis on individual stocks before, during, or after investing, which is the largest benefit of lazy stock index investing. On the other hand, it may be argued that your investment portfolio's potential for profit is larger the less daily management you do.

You did read that correctly.

Recognizing Risk

You also take on risk when you invest in stocks, which is why you get a return on your money. But in reality, there is always a certain amount of risk when dealing with money. Even with those crisp notes in your wallet, inflation could cause their value to decrease. A bag of gum, for instance, might cost $2 today. However, that cost might increase to $2.50 in a year. You can no longer buy that gum with your $2. That is a pretty condensed explanation of how inflation can reduce the purchasing power of your money.

In ETF investment, a "single point of failure"—a component within a group that, if it fails, could impair the remainder of the group—is less likely due to the diversification of a broad grouping of companies.

Using the energy market as an example, an ETF that invests in the whole industry would be less risky than purchasing the stock of a single energy business. Even if an energy company is successful, it is much more likely to collapse owing to subpar management, environmental violations, unqualified staff, or simply a very disastrous project. The possibility of this happening to the entire sector is, however, much smaller.

Can it Diversify Too Much?

An investor makes a bet when he purchases an investment property (a corporate share, an apartment, a private business), hoping that the value of that particular asset will rise, or that owning it would earn him an annual return, or ideally both. The investor is in a little bit of trouble if anything disastrous happens to that property, such as the bankruptcy of the only company leasing it or a sharp decline in the apartment's value.

For instance, you invested in an apartment building that offers a stunning view of the city from almost every window. The following day, a sign advertising a new skyscraper construction that will obscure half of the windows from that view is put up. The value of your initial investment simply decreased. Or you can say goodbye to your investment if you made a single business investment and something went wrong with it (bankruptcy, theft, product failure, etc.). Your portfolio's one-point failure risk is eliminated through index investing.

An ETF that tracks the market index, similar to the property example above, nearly totally overcomes this issue because when an investor purchases an ETF, they are essentially purchasing hundreds or even thousands of shares from numerous different companies. Therefore, it is likely that the investor would be completely unaware if one of the companies filed for bankruptcy, had other difficulties, or even suffered a quarter of significant losses.

The US market has served as the primary engine of global expansion for almost a century. How long will that continue? Most likely not. Furthermore, the real question isn't whether another country will take the reins, but rather when. However, for lazy investors like us, even considering this subject and its resolution is pointless. It can take hundreds of years for the torch to be passed from one abundant kingdom to the next. Empires crumble gradually, as history has shown generation after generation.

Let's spend a moment unpacking that. Has anyone who invested in British banks before the country's century-long historic slide regretted their choice, despite the fact that Britain's prominence on the international arena has undoubtedly declined over the years? No chance. The British Empire, which came to be described as a "empire on which the sun never sets," ruled over a third of the planet.

The British Empire began accelerating its conquests in the 16th century in order to take advantage of the resources and commercial routes of the countries they were assembling into the Commonwealth. Without the Internet, shares of financial institutions, transportation firms, and mining companies were sold in a manner similar to how they are today. Profits were booming for the British Empire at the expense of subjugated colonies in America, the Caribbean, and Africa. A new CEO named George Washington came into power following a 400-year financial celebration.

So what do historical geopolitical events have to do with us? In contrast to a century ago, we may now purchase the entire market with just two mouse clicks in the twenty-first century (or 2021 if you read this shortly after its first English printing). You can purchase ETFs that follow the global index if you're concerned about the collapse of the world's greatest economy (the US...so far). This makes it irrelevant whether the following superpower is Equatorial Guinea, Equatorial Guinea, or Russia. There you go, if we invest in the global market. Your portfolio is already performing well thanks to that new prosperous empire!

Irish-Based Etfs

The majority of the ETFs in my personal investing portfolio are Irish-based dividend-accruing ETFs. I developed this method after considering my own personal investment preferences, which include a desire for simplicity. Because of this, I only picked a small selection of Irish-based funds, each of which reinvested its dividends back into the fund. Simple, yes? As a result, I have less work to do and more time to write books, which I actually enjoy more than managing finances. Win-win!

Here is how it goes. Because Ireland permits dividend accumulation in funds and even offers tax incentives upon distribution of the dividend, several investment houses issue ETFs with Irish incorporation.

As of the time of writing, the tax agreement between the United States and Ireland permits a 10% dividend tax deduction. That reduces the original 25% dividend tax to a 15% tax. The drawback of saving money is that when it is sold, the investor must pay capital gains taxes on all profits made (25% at the time of writing), resulting in double taxation. Should we steer clear of the Irish funds in light of this? In no way!

Investors that are in it for the long term may actually prefer to pay double tax on dividends, if only to benefit from the Irish 10% tax cut on dividends over a number of years, given the enormous power of the compound interest rate. Although it may seem difficult, try reading it out loud twice.

It really is a question that only you can answer for yourself or with the help of a qualified tax counselor, whether or not it is wise to pay a reduced tax – paid twice — or pay the regular tax once. It necessitates a number of computations of personal income that we (clearly) aren't covered in this book. The first tax payment option listed above, double-but-reduced, is often more advantageous the longer you hold onto your investments.

Some of you may be concerned by this because you can presume that if the technology sector tanked, your entire investment portfolio would do the same.

Other investors could exclaim, "Give me more!" as they study the design of the graph charting the performance history of technology stocks on the NASDAQ.

Does the technology industry warrant the lazy investor's whole investment, or does this focus feel a little too constrained?

This is a worthwhile and significant question to pose. Since I am a passive investor, I am uninterested in market patterns because I lack the ability or desire to make future predictions. A 20% allocation to five assets in a portfolio is undoubtedly a substantial investment for an ETF. Our most popular purchases, however, are digital in today's world because a big amount of interpersonal communication is made possible by technology (mobile phones, chat applications, social media, etc.). But it's also possible that things will be radically different in the world of tomorrow. Most likely, that would also be reflected in our investing selections.

Pessimistic finance reporters were alarmed by the swift index graph correction that occurred during the COVID-19 crisis, commenting that "it was only the technology stocks that raised the entire index."

Why should we slothful investors be concerned with which stocks in an ETF boost the value of our investment? We already know that at any given time, only 4% of the index's shares are accountable for that rise. Instead than looking at moving stock charts, we should be doing much greater things.

The sloth hanging on a high branch of a tree, quietly chewing on some leaves while the world (or market) below it does its thing is analogous to the sluggish investor who invests in the stocks market using index-tracking ETFs. The graphs keep rising, falling, then rising once more. Reporters will keep shouting, "This time it's different!" while the economy keeps expanding and growing. There is no reason to think that this will change because it has happened in earlier centuries, long before you and I were born.

History rhymes, but it doesn't repeat itself.

- Mark Twain, purportedly

"Be modest. Accept your ignorance. Be lazy."

- Jonathan, a buddy of mine

Deferred taxes, a sweet dessert

All gains must be taxed in accordance with US tax regulations (and those of many other tax-collecting countries). The most typical is income tax, which you must pay to the government each year based on your earnings from employment. If you make less than $5,000 per year, you only pay up to 20% in taxes on your work income. However, the tax rate increases significantly if you make more than $5,000 per year, by roughly a third to half of your additional wage.

Capital gains, or income from the sale of assets (stocks, real estate, businesses, etc.), are also subject to taxation. There are two key distinctions between income tax and capital gains tax:

Everybody pays the same amount of capital gains tax, which is always 25% of profits. The payment is only made after the sale of the securities, and it is exclusively based on the profit.

Every pay period, or once a year if you are a business owner or independent contractor, you must pay income tax to the government. Your gross salary or other source of income is used to calculate this rate.

For instance, Jess invested $1,000 in an ETF that mimics the S&P 500 index. Jess made the decision to sell the investment after a year when its value climbed by 10%. She will receive a $1,100 return on her initial investment.

Prior to Jess leaving to enjoy herself, the investment firm will send $25, or precisely 25% of her gains, from the $100 she made to the state treasury.

Jess will only have $1,075 to spend on her celebration. However, things don't have to be this way. By deciding against selling the security, Jess can put off taking a part of her income. Until she ultimately decides to cash in her investment, the $25 she was meant to pay the investment house can continue to generate income for her.

Give Jess some time to reconsider her choice. Take your paycheck for the time being, hypothetically speaking, and consider what would occur if you invested that money now rather than paying hundreds or thousands of dollars in income tax and reaped the rewards afterwards. It is quite promising!

I adore the tax deferral method since it complements compound interest's basic idea so well. The tax deferral mechanism is something I genuinely adore and keep writing about. Here's another illustration:

Jonathan and Cary, two friends, made the decision to begin saving money jointly. Jonathan enjoys paying his taxes on time, however Cary finds the idea of paying taxes to be extremely unpleasant.

Each friend puts $10,000 into an ETF, which earns a 10% annual return.

Jonathan offered to redeem the money at the end of each year so that it may be reinvested because he enjoys paying his taxes so much!

After taking early retirement, Cary decides to leave the money alone so that it can grow tax-free for the following 20 years.

Increasing your sphere of expertise

The great man advised doing the following to widen your sphere of expertise: "Draw a circle around the companies you are familiar with, and then weed out those that don't meet the criteria for value, effective management, and minimal exposure to adversity. I would then choose each industry and gain some competence in six of them. The current conventional wisdom in any industry is of little significance to me. I would attempt to consider it. I would imagine that I had just inherited the business and that it was the only asset my family would ever possess when I was considering an insurance or paper firm. How would I utilize it? What am I contemplating? What causes me to worry? Whom do I compete against? Just who are my clients? By all means, speak with them. Find out how this specific company stacks up against the competition in terms of strengths and shortcomings. If you've done that, you might know more about the company than the management.

"Anyone who claims to be able to value all of life's stocks must have a very exaggerated view of their own abilities. It is not that simple. However, you may learn a lot about value if you spend your time concentrating on a few industries. Due to his inability to assess the companies involved due to staying inside his sphere of competence, Buffett will miss out on several profitable investments: "I missed the play in cellular. Cellular is after all outside of my area of expertise. A lifetime can be served by a circle of competence. Buffett was already interested in GEICO when he learned that his mentor, Benjamin Graham, was the company's chairman before Berkshire acquired the 49% of GEICO insurance that it didn't control in 1995. I put more than half of my net worth into GEICO when I was 20. When asked why he invested in this infamous roller-coaster industry, he responded, "Sometimes, it's a terrible business, and sometimes, it's a good business, but that's not quite often."

However, risk management is a crucial element in this situation: If you allow me to collect a sufficient premium, I will write life insurance in an emergency room. Recall that Buffett is renowned for his expertise in investing in insurance float, or the money that has been collected in premiums but not yet disbursed in claims. "Our principles are valid when applied to technology stocks, but we don't know how to do it," comments Buffett frequently. We want to come up here the following year and explain how we did it if we are going to waste your money. Bill Gates will undoubtedly use the same guidelines. He comprehends technology in the same manner that I comprehend Gillette or Coca-Cola. He undoubtedly seeks a margin of safety. He would undoubtedly treat it as if he were the owner of a company rather than merely stock. Therefore, our concepts apply to all technologies. Simply put, we can't handle it. We won't broaden the circle and will instead wait if we can't find anything within our sphere of expertise.

Charlie Munger offers some thoughts on the matter: The circle of competence is discussed. Three baskets should be available: in, out, and too tough. Put a lot of things in the "too hard" category. Buffett may have veered towards a higher level of technology due to his deepening connection and conversations with Bill Gates. (Gates joined the board of directors of Berkshire Hathaway in 2005; he resigned in 2020 "to devote more time to philanthropic priorities including global health and development, education, and in tackling climate change.") Buffett purchased 8.1% of TCA Cable TV and 6.8% of Great Lakes Chemical Corp. in 1999. Buffett invested $500 million in level three communications in 2002. This company runs the country's high-speed network for the transmission of voice and data communications.

The fact that level 3 was formed by a division of Omaha-based Peter Kiewit Sons Inc. and that Buffett's buddy and fellow board member Walter Scott Jr. served as its chairman contributed to Buffett's faith in the business that prompted him to spend that amount, among other things. You occasionally go beyond your area of expertise. Level 3 is one of those occasions, but I've staked my reputation on the populace, and I believe I comprehend it. There was a period when I was the subject of bets. Buffett kept growing his network by first purchasing the debt and preferred stock of Nextel. Then he bought TTL, a privately held top distributor of electromagnetic, interconnect, and passive components.

Think broad

Many years ago, during a Berkshire Hathaway annual meeting, Buffett tapped the podium to signal that the microphone was on and said, "Testing, one million... two million... three million. When I was managing an investing partnership, I conducted a research comparing all of our larger investments to the smaller investments. Always, the bigger investments outperformed the smaller ones. When making a significant decision, there is a threshold that must be crossed or attained that can cause you to be careless with smaller judgments. It is possible to claim, "I purchased 100 shares of this or that after hearing about it at a tea party the other night." There is a tendency to make minor decisions, and you might do so for less-than-stellar reasons. I am unable to participate in 50 or 75 items. You end up with a zoo if you invest in that way, like Noah's Ark. I like to invest significant sums of money in a select few items.

Buffett claims that small businesses can have excellent development, but he also states that a holding company the size of Berkshire should be looking for 747s, not model planes. I resemble a basketball trainer. I venture outside and search for 7-footers. I'm not interested if a guy approaches me and says, "I'm 5 foot 6, but you ought to see me handle the ball." The business, regardless of size, must deliver. A $10 million business that makes 15% of its revenue is preferable to a $100 million business that makes 5%.

Don't worry about math.

According to Buffett, he feels compelled to concur with those who assert that higher arithmetic ability is not necessary for successful investing because he never studied calculus: "I would have returned to distributing papers if calculus was necessary. I've never thought algebra was necessary. In essence, you're attempting to determine the worth of a business. It is true that you must divide by the total number of outstanding shares. I don't believe you would need to bring someone along to perform the calculations if you were going to go out and purchase a farm, an apartment building, or a dry cleaning business. The future earning potential of that business and how that compares to the asking price for the asset will determine whether you made the proper purchase or not. Read yearly reports, Ben Graham, and Phil Fisher, but avoid solving equations with Greek letters. Why is quantitative analysis so prevalent in scholarly and professional journals if higher math isn't necessary for choosing stocks?

Every clergy does it, Buffett said in response. If nobody is at the bottom, how can you be at the top? Buffett's non-mathematical mindset wasn't a natural fit. He created it after exhausting all other options: "I used to chart all different kinds of stocks, and the more numbers, the better." Buffett was enthralled by technology as a teenager. Due to this curiosity, Buffett, then 17 years old, published an article. "There was an article [in Barron's] stating that they would publish some of our statistical findings and pay $5 if we would email them an explanation of how we used their data. I published a piece describing my use of odd-lot figures. The only money I ever made from statistics was that $5.

admire thrift

"Whenever I read about a corporation doing a cost-cutting program, I can tell it's not a company that has a good understanding of expenses. Spurts are ineffective here. The genuinely good manager doesn't decide to cut costs when he wakes up in the morning any more than he decides to practice breathing when he wakes up. About 7% of the shares of the San Francisco-based Wells Fargo were owned by Berkshire Hathaway. Munger learned that Carl Reichardt, the CEO of Wells Fargo, had learned that one of his colleagues wanted to purchase a Christmas tree for the workplace. He should use his money to purchase it, Reichardt advised. "When we heard that, we bought more stock," claimed Munger. From its initial 13.66% stake, Berkshire now controls 8% of Wells Fargo.

To Buffett, being frugal starts at home. He made the following observation at the Berkshire annual meeting in 1996: "Your board has shed 100 pounds overall in the past year. They had to be attempting to survive off of their director's fees. In his foreword to Alan C. (ace) Greenberg's book "Memos From the Chairman" (Workman, 1996), Buffett admonished Bear Stearns employees not to squander money by quoting a fictional character named Haimchinkel Malintz Anaynikal. "Haimchinkel is my kind of man," Buffett remarked. "He's cheap, sharp, and outspoken. I only wish I had known him when I was younger and still discarded paper clips due to my ignorance. However, it's never too late, therefore I now adhere to and advocate for his beliefs. Buffett said that the necessity for economy and the pursuit of quality need not be mutually exclusive when discussing programming at ABC:

"The thing is, better shows don't cost that much more than lousy shows." The cost of airing sports programming might also be reduced: "I guess that the quality of football would have remained the same if we had paid 20% less for the football rights. All football players would simply make a little less money overall. Ty Cobb was paid $20,000 a year to play. In the end, the players will bear a big portion of the cost if there is 20% less funding for sports programming. Buffett used frugality in his financial dealings as well. In 1993, he and former capital cities/SBC chairman Thomas Murphy collaborated with Susan Lucci on various episodes of the ABC television soap opera "All my Children." Each of Buffett and Murphy received $300 for their performances. When Murphy received his check, he declared, "I'm going to frame this." Buffett proclaimed, "I'm going to find the stub."

Sign up with AA (Airlines Anonymous)

Buffett wrote off $268.5 million in 1995, representing 75% of his $385 million investment in USAir. Since September 1994, the dividend on the shares of 9.25% has not been paid. Buffett was looking for a buyer for the convertible preferred stock in the spring of 1996: "That was senior security stocks. It was a mistake, but we didn't choose common equity as a fantastic company. There aren't many excellent companies in the world. In a speech in North Carolina, Buffett highlighted why airlines are not a good investment: "The amazing point is that the airline transport company in the United States hasn't produced any money if you go back to the time from Kitty Hawk to the net. Imagine yourself watching this guy go up at Kitty Hawk and suddenly having the realization that one day, tens of millions of others would be doing the same thing all over the world. We would all get along better because of that.

Even after investing several billions of dollars, the net return to owners for the entire airline business would be less than zero if you had owned it all. If there was a capitalist there, he ought to have shot Wilbur down. One tiny stride forward for humanity and one enormous step backward for capitalism. Buffett says he was temporarily insane when he bought USAir. How will he defend himself from a future assault? "So now I have this 800 number and if I ever have the temptation to buy an airline stock, I dial this number and say my name is Warren and I'm a "aircoholic," he said. On the other end, this guy starts to belittle me. Buffett still battles his passion for the aviation industry while being a member of Airlines Anonymous. His USAir venture did not turn up nicely. Then, in a fit of shame, he purchased a corporate plane that he dubbed "The Indefensible." Later, following the Salomon brothers incident, he changed the name to "The Defensible."

When he discovered NetJets, a new object of aviation adoration, in 1998, his love affair with the plane came to an end. "I'm not flying "The Defensible," which is the very defensible. It didn't make sense for me to control the entire strategy. I did it because I thought it was my only choice. It makes no sense to pay for four or five times the capacity that you require. One destroyer is not enough for someone with a full fleet of aircraft, just as they would require a whole array for a navy with just one sort of boat. Every single day, I'm on a different mission. I have a choice of 11 different aircraft types for a flight that will be 300 miles in the United States, 1,200 miles, or over Europe. In order to purchase a portion of a certain plane and use it or trade it for a set number of flying hours each year, customers of NetJets can purchase fractional ownership of an aircraft. Warren and Charlie, who usually take commercial coaches, use the service because it's so convenient.

Returning to commercial planes after having traveled on NetJets is like going back to touching hands. The privately held business was purchased by Berkshire for $725 million in shares and cash. Buffett's unfortunate aviation karma unfortunately reappeared. Due to a lack of appropriate equipment, high operating costs (fuel), and its presence in European markets, NetJets' profitability declined. NetJets experienced pre-tax losses of $10 million in 2004 and $80 million in 2005. Buffett held onto the belief that the business would reverse course and begin turning a profit. Rich Santulli, one of the most energizing managers I've ever seen, would therefore fix our revenue/expense dilemma, he wrote in 2005. But he won't do it in a way that degrades the NetJets travel experience. We both share a commitment to providing customers with unmatched levels of service, security, and safety. While NetJets' performance did indeed improve in 2006, it was still negative.

In Europe, it was profitable, and Buffett said that the fleet value was far higher than that of NetJets' three main rivals. People in the airline business frequently remind anxious passengers that the pilot genuinely cares about getting them to the airport safely since his life is on the line along with theirs. Buffett flies NetJets for around 225 hours a year, and his family flies for an additional 550 hours. Therefore, other customers like Tiger Woods, Calvin Klein, and Kathie Lee Gifford may rest easy knowing that they will get the same superior staff and aircraft as the Buffetts do.

Invest in books' stocks

Buffett's preferred method of articulating intrinsic value and margin of safety has literary aspects. In the words of Buffett, his favorite businesses are "wonderful castles, encircled by deep, perilous moats, where the boss inside is a decent and honest guy. The leader generates gold inside, but he doesn't hoard it all for himself. Ideally, the genius inside gives the castle its strength; the most is permanent and works as a potent deterrent to those considering an attack. We want exceptional organizations with dominant positions, whose franchise is challenging to replicate, and who have a lot of staying power or a sense of permanence. To defend yourself against the competitor who will provide [your product] for a penny less, you need a moat in business. When Buffett remarked in 1969: "When I buy a stock, I conceive of it in terms of buying a whole company; just as if I were buying the store down the street, I make a real-world examination of my favorite storybook stock transaction.

I would want to know everything if I were buying the store. Take a look at what Walt Disney was worth in the first half of 1966 on the stock market. Considering that Snow White, the Swiss Family Robinson, and some other cartoons that had been written off the books were worth that much on their own, the $53 price per share didn't appear to be cheap, but on that basis, you could buy the entire company for $80 million. In addition, you had

Disneyland and Walt Disney (a genius) as a partner. Following the 1996 merger of CAP cities/ABC with Disney, Berkshire retained a significant stake in the company: "Owning the movie Snow White is like owning an oil field. It creeps back in after you pump it out and sell it. Remember that Disney has since learned that the Snow White movie can be rereleased every seven years. Mickey Mouse is another example. "The nice thing about the mouse is that he doesn't have an agent," says Mickey. The mouse is yours. His is yours.

After management issues at the kids' entertainment park began, Berkshire would finally sell its Disney stock.

Discover exemplary businesses

There will come a time when a fool will run a firm, so you should invest in one that anyone can manage.

Any firm would have a variety of circumstances that will occur next week, next month, next year, and so on. But being in the correct industry is what's actually crucial. Coca-Cola, which went public in 1919, is a prime example. At first, they priced the stock at $40 per share. The following year, it was $19 instead. After World War I, sugar prices substantially changed. If you had purchased the stock when it first went public, you would have lost half of your investment after a year, but if you had held onto same share today and had reinvested all of your dividends, it would be worth about $1.8 million. Wars and depressions have occurred. The cost of sugar has been fluctuating up and down. Numerous events have taken place. How much more beneficial is it for us to consider whether the prudent is likely to maintain itself and its economy than to attempt to consider whether to enter or exit the stock?

"Say you wanted to invest but you were leaving for a ten-year trip. You already knew everything and there was nothing you could do to change it. What are your thoughts about it? In terms of certainty, I came up with anything where I knew the market would continue to expand, where I knew the leader would hold onto the top spot, and where I knew there would be significant unit growth. Simply put, I had no familiarity with Coke.

"Charlie (Munger) made me concentrate on the merits of a great company with tremendously growing earning power, but only when you are sure about it, unlike Texas Instruments or Polaroid, where the earning power was speculative,"

When no one else was interested, Buffett once explained to Phillip Smith, the former president of General Foods, why he was buying the company's stock: "You have strong brand names, you're selling three times earnings when other food companies are selling at six to seven times earnings, and you're loaded with cash. Someone else will know what to do with it if you are unsure.

After Philip Morris bought General Foods, it was combined with Kraft Food. Altria is the new name for Philip Morris.

"A great company will be great for at least 25 years," the adage goes.

The fact that, after making a purchase, an investor merely needs to sit back and trust the company's managers to do their duties is one rationale for investing in good companies (apart from rapid growth). Buffett already held stakes in at least six insurance firms, a trading stamp business, a chain of women's apparel stores, a confectionery company, a significant piece of Berkshire Hathaway, an Illinois bank, an Omaha weekly newspaper, and a number of other businesses in 1973. I can almost do it with my hands in my pockets, he said modestly to a reporter. I have a rather simple life.

"I advise everyone who works for our company to do just two things in order to succeed: first, think like an owner, and second, promptly inform us of any negative information. Concerning the wonderful news, there is no need for concern.

Sometimes junk bonds can be gold.

Buffett said, in response to a question, "I think they'll live up to their name." When questioned later on why he spent $139 million on junk bonds issued by the high-risk Washington Public Power Supply System (WPPSS, often known as Whoops), Buffett responded, "We don't make decisions based on ratings. We would hand over our money to Moody's and Standard & Poor's if we wanted them to manage it.

Remarks: A fixed 16.3% tax-free yield was offered on the bonds that didn't default, generating an annual return of $22.7 million.

Since then, Buffett has profited from investments in RJR Nabisco, Chrysler Finance, Texaco, Time Warner, and Amazon.com bad bonds. No, I'm not an engineer. Even when I flick the switch, I have no idea why the light comes on. But

I am skilled at choosing garbage bonds. Buffett noted that there are some similarities between investing in equities and buying garbage on auction sites in Berkshire's 2002 annual report: "Both activities require us to make price-value calculations and scan hundreds of securities to find the very few with attractive reward/risk ratios." But he has very different expectations for these two types of investments. He anticipates profits from all of his stock purchases, but not from his purchases of trash bonds: "We are dealing with businesses that have far higher margins when we buy junk bonds. These companies frequently operate in sectors with low capital returns while being heavily indebted. The caliber of their management staff is occasionally in doubt.

We anticipate that we will occasionally experience significant losses in junk issues since management may have interests that are directly at odds with those of debt holders. However, we have performed admirably in this regard thus far. Berkshire owns numerous fixed-income and bond interests, both directly and indirectly (via insurance subsidiaries), according to Charlie Munger. Therefore, he is not bothered by Berkshire's investment in so-called "junk". Munger replied, "I love to see it done as long as Warren is doing it." "Over the years, we have made a few hundred million pretax dollars doing that without much risk or fuss," he continued. We now have that additional category.

Be aware of franchise value

Buffett compares franchise value to a moat encircling a castle of commerce. He used Gillette as an example, saying: "There are 21 billion razor blades used worldwide each year. While just 30% of them are Gillette's, 60% of them are, in terms of value. In certain nations (like Scandinavia and Mexico, for instance), they hold 90% of the market. When a product has been around for as long as shaving and you find a firm that consistently innovates by creating better razors, plus you have the distribution power and the position in people's thoughts, you know you have a company with franchise value. You may get a great shaving experience by doing it every day, which is something I hope you do. Men are not prone to moving around in those kinds of situations. You drift off to sleep with the thought that there are 2.5 billion men who have hair that grows while they are asleep. At Gillette, nobody has difficulties falling asleep.

Remarks: In 2004, Gillette and Proctor & Gamble amalgamated, giving Berkshire a 3% stake in P & G.

Another illustration of the idea of franchise value is Hershey Bars: "If you walk into a store and the clerk says, 'I don't have Hershey's, but I have an unmarked chocolate bar that the store owner recommends.If you're willing to walk across the street to purchase a Hershey bar, or if you'll spend a nickel more for the [Hershey] bar than the unmarked bar, or something similar, then that is franchise value. Also available is the lover test. Sometimes a low cost isn't the main concern: "You are aware of this. On Valentine's Day, they won't return home and hand their significant other two pounds of chocolates. I chose the low offer. It really isn't effective. The franchise value of Coca-Cola is the highest of any corporation in the world. "You're lucky if you come up with one solid business concept in your lifetime. The best huge company in the world, in essence, is Coca-Cola. It possesses the strongest brand in the entire planet. It is offered for a remarkably affordable price.

It is well-liked worldwide, and nearly every country sees an increase in per capita consumption every year. There isn't anything else like it. The moat of franchise power provides effective defense: "A takeover [of Coca-Cola] would be like the bombing of Pearl Harbor." Buffett has invested in businesses encountering severe financial troubles more than time (including

American Express in 1963 and GEICO insurance), a circumstance that has no bearing on the franchise value of those businesses: "Like American Express, GEICO was worth a ton of money even though it had no net worth; yet, because of this, it might be shut down the following day. But knowing that the net worth would be there made me happy. The truth is that many insurance firms would have raised the net value for the ownership of it. We would have mounted it.

The importance of temperament

September 2008 saw the world undergo a permanent change in less than two weeks. Stock markets, individual investors, and international governments were all plunged in a financial panic. Investors were forced to hold on for dear life as stock markets fell sharply. Volatility was the buzzword of the day, with palpable worries reaching a new peak as markets hit fresh lows. Stock prices, market morale, and consumer confidence all declined. The Dow Jones industrial average dropped below 10,000 points by the next month for the first time since 2004. The Standard & Poor's 500 indices had a 42% collapse over the prior year on October 9, 2008, wiping out years of gains. By October 9, 2008, it had fallen below 8,600. Before the year was over, this and numerous other business disasters occurred. Warren Buffett, who had witnessed the end of the world seemingly many times before, is unmoved.

Even he probably couldn't escape the hourly barrage of images of Wall Street traders who appeared scared, frantic, or just resigned to it all. He heard the loud voices on TV. When this intense panic hit, he did what any sane person would have done: he started buying valuable equities at steep discounts. He invested $20 billion in businesses including General Electric and Goldman Sachs. Looking past the situation required a certain mentality. Warren Buffett refrained from selling in a panic. He maintained his composure, evaluated the circumstance, and took action with confidence that was supported by years of experience. He urged others to follow suit, assuring them that we had previously overcome difficult circumstances and come out on top each time. The best time to buy equities, he further reminded investors, was when everyone was exiting the market, leaving a wealth of deals available for the taking. To suggest that this was an easy mentality to embrace during this frenzy would be a massive understatement.

Most investors and money managers can only dream about Warren Buffett's lengthy and successful career in the financial industry, and many would certainly kill for it. He has been researching businesses, making investments in the best of them, and accumulating fortune for almost five decades. He has no equal in the world. However, Buffett's unique temperament is what actually characterizes him, what makes him the investor he is today, and what has distinguished him from all those other investors throughout the years. In the world of investing, temperament is demonstrated by how much your decisions are influenced by your emotions, leading you, for instance, to buy, panic, and sell earlier than you should. whether you assume excessive risk. Whether you're frantically transferring money in and out of stocks without ever understanding what the company doing them does. Whether you allow market fluctuations to frighten you to the point where you become paralyzed, or whether you look at falling prices and find chances.

"Temperament, not intelligence, is the most crucial characteristic for an investor. You require a temperament that neither enjoys being with or against the crowd greatly.

Once you have an IQ above 125, investing success is not correlated with IQ. Once you have average intelligence, you need the temperament to restrain the urges that cause other investors to lose money.

The good news is that you can develop a disposition that is more long-term oriented. You can learn to invest more serenely. You can reduce your risk-taking by changing from a speculator to an investor mindset. Your financial performance will increase as you develop emotional self-control and a disposition like to Warren Buffett.

10 Pointers You Should Consider

For some, making stock market investments appears like the worst course of action. Many people "get burned by the market" because they commit frequent errors. Follow the advice given here if you don't want to lose your money, despise this lovely market for making money, and tell everyone about your negative experience.

Put risk management safeguards in place before making a trade. First is risk management. How much of your capital you are willing to lose is up to you. Some people won't lose more than a ratio of 2:1, which entails losing 1% of their investment and making 2% on whatever trades they make. If you invest $100, you could only be ready to risk $10 because you're hoping to profit at least $20. There are things like stop loss, trailing stop loss, and placing profit orders in addition to figuring out your risk/reward ratio. If the market moves against you, these orders will safeguard your position.

assemble a varied portfolio. The saying, "Never put all your eggs in one basket," couldn't be more accurate when it comes to the stock market. You may feel somewhat safe if you invested all of your money with Google. Google is enduring and getting stronger, but what if a catastrophe occurs that upsets the stock market's equilibrium altogether? The world's leading digital corporation and search engine, Google, is abruptly eliminated from existence. Your entire capital would be lost. Spreading your money out is significantly preferable to investing it all in a single, long-term stable stock. You can never tell what might occur.

Invest in markets you are familiar with. Some experts would advise you to invest in anything that is popular. The media, for instance, frequently lists hot stocks and those that are anticipated to affect the market. Warren Buffet, though, summed it up well when he noted that he does not overextend himself into fields in which he lacks expertise. He continues to do what he knows. Additionally, you should stick to the industries that you are most familiar with or that you can learn about without becoming lost. Say you're employed in the medical field. You are aware of the brands that sell these goods as well as the hottest drugs and electronic accessories. Start there, then broaden your horizons.

Read as much as you can. 80% of Warren Buffet's waking hours are spent reading. You should read as much as you can if you plan to make stock market investing your career or primary source of income. Newspapers, periodicals, RSS feeds, and all other sources of current business news should be easily accessible to you. The more you learn about the industries you are interested in investing in, the better you will be able to decide quickly when a stock is ready for an investment.

Recognize that news media, social media, and the media generally aim to influence the market. An investor trying to pique your interest in their position by speaking on CNBC. The greater the volume and fulfillment of the prophecy the media expert was addressing, the more individuals who invest in a position that has been featured in the media. However, this does not always happen. A second expert may have a different prediction, a corporation may act contrary to expected news, or not enough interest may be seen in the stock to cause the market price to move in the direction predicted by the expert.

Rely on the results of your research, technical indicators, and business news. As opposed to looking at one news site or listening to one news expert, looking at the overall picture for a company's stock can give you excellent recommendations and indicators. When looking for individual stocks to buy, you must always do your own research.

Be a machine. Our judgment is clouded by emotions. They often cause us to react hastily and unreasonably. You must trade on the stock market as though it were an automated machine. You make use of all the research you've done, but you don't experience any feelings of anticipation, letdown, or the "gamblers' high." Instead, you continue on to the next deal after each one is finished, regardless of whether it was a win or a loss.

Be businesslike with your investments. To make money, you would invest in a firm. The same holds true for investment. Spend money on educational resources, seminars, tutorials, and charting software for the stock market. One charting software program that offers a variety of lessons, webinars, seminars, and training materials is InvestTools. You can use this training option to access paper money accounts as well. You can get the knowledge you need to make investments for greater profit by making an investment in tools like these.

Be tolerant. There will be instances when investing in the market is not a good idea. Significant news can disrupt the market as a whole. For instance, the UK said that the majority of voters approved the proposal to quit the EU. The repercussions were felt on that day on the London stock exchange. As a result of the announcement, investors withdrew. In order to prevent another Great Depression, the US stock exchange has been shut down on several times. Wait when the market isn't worthwhile for investment.

Pick a broker after conducting thorough investigation. Brokers charge varying fees and have various account restrictions. A single broker may charge $5 for both the opening and closing trades. A other broker might charge twice as much. Some businesses will bill you $10 for the open and closure together.

The Fundamentals Of Buying Penny Stocks

The foundation is the first thing to lay when building a house, and the same is true while learning or building anything. Understanding the foundation is one of the most important parts of laying the groundwork for your success in penny stock investing. Naturally, your next goal is to create for yourself an empire of trading expertise and hoped-for profits. However, you have to begin somewhere, right? Making the best trading decisions occasionally requires stripping everything back to the essentials.

What Drives The Stock Market

Although there is some risk associated with the stock market, it has been repeatedly demonstrated that if a disciplined approach is taken, then it is undoubtedly one of the finest ways to increase a person's net worth.

A typical marketplace where people can purchase and sell shares of firms is the stock market. Stock prices are determined by supply and demand in the market, and stocks themselves signify ownership in a corporation. It may also be known as an equity or share. As a result, a share's value is based on the volume of activity generated by both buyers and sellers. Stocks also serve as a means of claiming a portion of a company's earnings as well as some of its assets, which are the things the company actually owns.

Businesses frequently desire to raise more money than a bank loan would permit. They also don't want the responsibility of having to pay back a bank with a hefty interest rate. This is a typical justification for issuing shares: to boost scalability without incurring excessive debt. Raising capital is a terrific method to accelerate a company's growth and earnings, but occasionally a company does require a lot of money to get off the ground. The main justification for firms issuing shares is capital expansion. You do need to generate money quickly and effectively if you want to expand at a faster rate.

Stock comes in two basic varieties: common and favored. The primary distinction between the two that does exist typically has to do with voting rights. The right to vote and speak at meetings, including those where the board of directors or even the auditors are up for election, belongs to common shareholders. Despite not having these voting rights, preferred shares are treated more favorably than common shares and are more likely to receive dividends or assets in the event of a firm liquidation.

Stock market

In actual life, the stock exchange functions similarly to a thrift shop. Existing shareholders can sell their shares on this marketplace to prospective buyers. On this platform, buyers communicate with shareholders rather than the companies directly. The fact that public corporations typically don't have as much control over who buys their shares is highlighted by this.

Announcing Shares

When a business first starts out, it will require a significant amount of capital, which it can obtain through activities like a bank loan. However, why take on debt when you can sell your shares to the general public? This is typically accomplished through an initial public offering (IPO), which can alter the company's official status. Assuming the business is successful, the IPO typically gives early investors the chance to cash out and the opportunity to get sizable profits.

The company's shares may vary until they are actually listed on a stock exchange as traders and investors attempt to determine the worth.

How to Set Share Prices

The auction process is the most typical setting where the price of a share usually tends to be set. Here are the bids and offers to buy or sell the shares made by buyers and sellers, respectively. In contrast to the offer, which is the price the seller is willing to accept as payment, the bid represents the price that buyers are willing to pay. The average price at which shares are typically sold depends on supply and demand.

The Price-Earnings or even (PE) ratio is the most popular technique for valuing a stock among the numerous alternative ratios or metrics that can be utilized. This is a fantastic approach to learn more about the analytics side of the business's financial sector.

Returns on Investment for Stocks

ROIs, also referred to as returns on stock investments, calculate the profit or loss associated with a particular investment. The usual way to do this is to take the final investment amount and deduct it from the initial cost you invested. It goes without saying that you have profited if your response is positive. If the response is no, on the other hand, you have lost. Additionally, since this will increase your earnings, you can figure out how many dividends you have received.

There are typically two categories for stocks. One is market capitalization, which is the entire value of the shares of a corporation traded on the market. The Global Industry Classification Standard is used to categorize equities by sector in the other. The MSCI and Standard & Poor's established and introduced the Global Industry Classification Standard as an industry taxonomy in 1999. This was applied to the world of finance.

Where to Trade Penny Stocks

You might now find it useful to know what direct sources to seek out. Some of the top markets are listed below. You must realize that while each has particular benefits to offer, there are also drawbacks to each because there isn't a flawless system out there. The best course of action is for you to choose what works for you and what dangers you are actually willing to accept. Some of the exchanges mentioned aren't even suggested; rather, they're listed to raise awareness about what novice and even seasoned traders should think about avoiding.

Small-Cap Market on NASDAQ

NASDAQ Capital Market, formerly known as NASDAQ Small Cap Market until the year 2005, primarily lists small-cap companies, but its name was changed to reflect a significant change in focus. The businesses on this list are looking to raise funds. It implies that small businesses could expand through the NASDAQ listing without experiencing a significant burden from being listed on this exchange.

The benefits include that you can invest after business hours and during extended trading hours as opposed to the NYSE, which can only handle trading during business hours. NASDAQ's after hours trading allows you to occasionally trade till eight o'clock in the evening.

Using this platform, you can trade from the comfort of your home using internet automation. Having online access to this platform eliminates the requirement for the investor to administer trades on their behalf. Instead, the investor can handle a majority of the trading duties themselves. This does provide you greater freedom and control over the decisions you wish to make, though, to a certain extent.

Though many of the listings on Nasdaq are known to be extremely volatile, it does not have the same amount of respect as other stock exchanges. Additionally, keep in mind that penny stocks have their own drawbacks. OTC-BB

Over-the-counter bulletin boards, or OTB-BBs, allow you to secure deals through a broker-dealer network. This displaces the centralized exchange hubs and can involve derivatives like shares, debt instruments, and other financial products. For those who would rather remain anonymous, cutting out the middleman is always advantageous, and you can locate many stocks that are not listed on the active exchanges. Over-the-counter equity securities are the usual name for these shares of stock.

Working in the OTC market requires more caution because of the laxer security and regulatory standards. This indicates that scams and unsuccessful companies happen regularly.

Amex

Amex is a recognizable, international financial brand with millions of employees and billions of dollars in annual sales. It is well-liked and fairly modern.

Considering its lengthy history, Amex is a reasonably reliable option but is never a 100% certainty. Revenue is still increasing steadily, and steps are being taken to keep up with other expanding markets. Additionally, a stronger digital focus is beginning to emerge.

The outcomes of the year's earnings have, however, slightly declined, and this can be fairly worrying for investors because Amex is trailing the competition. Additionally, it has numerous difficulties in its role as a card issuer, and employing this platform results in only modest dividend yields. All of these things need to be taken into account.

Markets in Canada

The Canadian stock markets have been performing extremely well, and they have a strong financial industry and access to many resources. Even when the economy and situation seem secure, it is necessary to approach them objectively.

First off, transactions are now doing well in Canada and the Canadian dollar is strong. As was previously said, Canada has a very stable banking system. There are many tools available, particularly in businesses and stock exchanges. This makes buying penny stocks in this industry more alluring.

Be warned, however, that due to a lack of diversity, several areas of this industry suffer from a severe lack of resources. Furthermore, given the size of the market, it may be advisable to diversify your portfolio into other markets even if you were to contemplate investing. Though it is powerful, there is a currency risk as well. The economy and Canadian banks will feel a lot of pressure if inflation rates start to climb quickly.

Avoid Pink Sheets Penny Stocks!

This is just given here to highlight the fact that it is not at all advised. Since pink sheet stocks serve as a quotation service rather than an exchange for OTC trading, they have historically been regarded as solid investments. The fundamental issue, however, is that pink sheet stocks are scarcely traded and have little liquidity. Many of the companies that use penny stocks on the pink sheet are completely worthless. Simply put, investing in pink sheets penny stocks is not worth the risk because you are much more likely to lose money on this market than to win it.

Dollar Stocks Directly from the Businesses

Investing directly with the company removes the safety of regulations that are still in place despite being penny stocks. There is absolutely no guarantee of a fair valuation, and you are far more likely to get scammed or ripped off. There are too many companies that are scraping by the edge of their teeth and the investments coming in from ignorant bystanders hoping to get some return. The chances are very slim, and your money is not adequately protected.

Penny Stocks Over the Phone

Just a horrible concept all around. First of all, it is impossible to accurately check who you are speaking to over the phone, and secondly, it is probably a hoax. A person should not have to explain why trading penny stocks over the phone should never be considered.

Buying Penny Stocks: Basic Elements

When purchasing penny stocks, there are a few fundamental components you should be aware of and inspect. To complete your order, you will provide the following information.

The ticker system comes first. You'll likely need to know the company's name, which is as follows. Next, you'll need to be familiar with the market where penny stocks are traded. After all, it is best to know where to work on the exchanges if you want to target a particular corporation.

You must also choose how many penny stocks you want to purchase. Normally, this is regarded as the number of shares and the amount you have allocated to your budget. For instance, if the company offers shares for $0.50 a share and you have $2000, you should order roughly 4000 shares if you plan to purchase them all at that price.

Additionally, you should decide on a market or limit pricing. This is for trade orders or shares whose price you aren't entirely certain. It is advisable to limit the price to ensure that the trade price will be carried out. You won't pay any more for those shares if, for instance, it is set at $0.70 per share. So, if they are asking an absurdly high price for it, you don't get taken advantage of by the business.

The length of your order is also up to you. Market orders typically don't need a term of any kind, but if you're prepared to wait for your share to reach the perfect price, you can have your order filled as soon as it enters the trading floor.

On the other hand, limit orders require a duration, and you will also receive a second limit order duration.

The cost in its entirety should then be calculated. It is best to take into account not just the share price but also any commission fees and other possible levies. Again, having a budget and an estimate of the costs will help you avoid any unpleasant surprises.

You will then require an open order. This is the time frame in which your order is still open and will not expire. If you have an online brokerage account, checking your open orders should be simple. This is the best course of action. It is a great way to check and see the shares you have purchased and the price you have paid for them.

Selling penny stocks involves the same elements as buying stocks, just in a matter of slight reversal. Instead of paying for them, you are obviously selling them.

Choose A Stock Broker

Selecting your stockbroker is crucial since they act as the intermediary, and there are two categories of stockbrokers you should be aware of. You should pick different stockbrokers based on your goals because they vary in a few key areas.

The discount broker comes first. Of course, you pay less for them, but typically that just means they do as you say. You'll have to conduct your own research, and your choice will have no bearing on them.

The full-service broker is the second. They charge a larger cost, but they spend more time advising you, providing you directions, and creating a portfolio plan for you. Those clients that have larger portfolios and are prepared to pay greater commission costs will benefit from this more than others.

broker standards

How do you select the best broker for your needs? For this, you can do a number of things. You must first decide what you need for yourself. It does depend on your circumstances and position. Despite any inclination to add variety, it is also preferable to have just one broker rather than three or more.

You must examine commission costs to ensure that they are within your means and that the broker's order execution turnaround time is acceptable to you. Since not every broker is familiar with penny stocks' rules, you'll obviously want a broker that is reputable and is knowledgeable about them.

You must consider the broker's availability in case problems emerge and the caliber of client care. It will be quite tough to collaborate with them if their customer support is problematic.

It's also a good idea to look into a customer's research and toolkit. What tools do they have at their disposal, and how effectively are they able to keep up with the trends? Although staying current is crucial, not all brokers follow this philosophy.

Models Of Business In The Metaverse

The Metaverse will have some specific business models.

Vox store

In the meta world, different materials and pieces of equipment are used than in the real world. For instance, voxels make up the majority of cryptovoxels, as well as the wearables and structures. Vox will be required for Metaverse users to display their avatars or dress up on special events. As a result, some groups of people actively seek out vox, usually during vox walks.

The NFT art auction

The Metaverse's art gallery currently has the most business models available. Most artists and several groups of related artists were among the first people in the Metaverse interested in developing a business model. Among them are the BCA Gallery, the Chijin Pavilion, and a few Korean painters. This group of individuals contributed to the promotion of the gallery, which is a staple of the Metaverse's economic system.

The company providing metauniverse creation

Some landlords have a lot of land, but they don't always have the time to build on it. Some landlords own businesses and are looking to expand their brands by hiring a highly skilled individual or team. This demand has sparked interest from the metaverse construction industry, including businesses like voxel architects and meta estates. The four primary structures in the Metaverse were mostly designed by voxel artists.

Advertising

The adverts may be the cause of any traffic you encounter when playing in the Metaverse. The services for metaverse billboards offer billboards for advertising in the metaverse. There are a lot of billboards displayed there. The cryptovoxels of the metaverse contain about 250 billboards. These advertisements provide opportunities for income.

leasing for real estate

There is a large market for purchasing and selling digital real estate. You can also rent to others. Since there are so many locations with ample plots, some people choose to spend their money in land rather than building. Let's say that these people are willing to sell or lease the lands to anyone who has a business plan and a unique structure they want to construct there. It's going to make sense. That is a fantastic transactional method.

immersive experience with the meta world

The ability to fully immerse oneself in a virtual environment allows users to forget about their immediate surroundings and concentrate on their current surroundings. There are projects for immersive gaming experiences everywhere. You can become completely engrossed in the game, chase the large fish into the water, and even scale tall structures. The Metaverse's developers ought to make an effort to fund these immersive initiatives to increase participant engagement.

Internet KTV

KTV is a genuine social outlet. Customers will spend money to participate in this social connection. However, offline KTV is only available at specific locations, making it very difficult for those thousands of miles away to attend an event to take part in this K song. There are people from all around the world who join the Metaverse and stay there permanently.

game object

Another business model needs to be replaced here. These games should be simple to integrate into the meta-universe environment. For instance, you can tell it's a blockchain gaming platform by looking at the sandboxes. On that blockchain, game developers can employ voxel assets and other tools. The game might possibly be included in the items that will be included in the Metaverse. Players will have the opportunity to learn what it's like to both invest and play games.

Service provider for data

In the Metaverse, as in the real world, everything is connected to data. When information about the land the landlord owns becomes available, the person who wants to buy the land will also be interested in learning more details about the property. There will be a wide variety of occupations available to inhabitants once the Metaverse has been properly established. Products like amusement park designer, architect, 3D scanner, and venue operator for the metaverse are anticipated to emerge.

Investing in the Metaverse: How to Do It

Humans will always be accessible on virtual platforms, with the ability to travel about the virtual world utilizing avatars and digital objects. And instead of using fiat money to make purchases, individuals will switch to using cryptocurrencies like ethereum and Bitcoin (BTC). There will probably be a ton of commercial opportunities created by the metaverse. And it might be among the top locations for investments.

You are good to go if you enjoy investing and are probably accustomed to the processing. Additionally, you should strive to learn more about investing if you don't already know anything about it. Although the idea of a metaverse does not yet seem feasible, there are several chances for people to indirectly support the development of the metaverse we have been discussing. This claim is supported by Bloomberg Intelligence's prediction that the Metaverse market would reach $800 billion by 2024, making it the best sector to invest in. Let's examine the manner in which the

Metaverse can be included into your set of financial portfolios.

Mt. Gox stocks

One of the various options for investing in the Metaverse is this. By purchasing your metaverse stocks, you can invest in this. All shares that can be traded publicly by businesses involved in the development of the metaverse are referred to as metaverse stock. Facebook is one of the businesses from which you can purchase stock. Facebook is an option if you're looking for ways to invest in the Metaverse. According to Mark Zuckerberg, the business should be referred to as a metaverse firm rather than a social media corporation. Facebook recently unveiled its newly acquired smart glasses in collaboration with Ray-Ban to develop them for augmented reality. There are numerous other firms to invest in, so you might opt against investing solely in Facebook. including Microsoft, Roblox, Walt Disney, Amazon, and Nvidia, as well as the Unity software.

Exchange-traded funds in the metaverse

Another investment option is this.
Investors can experience the metaverse
in a variety of ways. By acquiring a
metaverse ETF, theta keeps increasing.
The securities in an exchange-traded
fund can be exchanged on an exchange
just like stocks. The EFT for the
metaverse stock enables a variety of
people to invest in some of the
businesses that wish to create the
metaverse or who are working hard to
do so in the future.

The Roundhill Ball metaverse ETF is an
illustration of that kind of metaverse
business. People can invest and benefit

from the Metaverse thanks to it. Investors have access to firms like Microsoft, Nvidia, Tencent, Roblox, Amazon, and Unity thanks to the Roundhill investment.

NFTS Metaverse

Most blockchain powered by Metaverse will most likely employ NTFS. The adoption and growth of the Metaverse will largely depend on cryptoassets. Why?

You will need them for the Metaverse in order to enable users to easily transport each avatar they built as well as other virtual assets from one location to another. Many different things can be represented digitally using NTFS, which are digital assets. such as collectibles, works of art, and in-game stuff.

online currency tokens

The virtual world tokens are another electronic tokens that are related to the virtual reality sector. Tokens from virtual worlds can be used by users to buy land and avatars in the Metaverse. An illustration of a token from a virtual environment is the metaverse index. It provides its owners with details on various tokens obtained from cryptocurrency initiatives that focus on particular industries like non-fungible tokens, online gaming, and virtual worlds. As a result, the metaverse index token works similarly to a metaverse you could use to trade cryptocurrencies.

Another virtual reality application that enables users to buy land, chat with one another, and even play games is decentraland. With a virtual land reflected on the Ethereum blockchain, it is the largest virtual world in the non-fungible tokens market. There are two distinct tokens used in decentraland:

LAND and MANA. The non-fungible token known as "LAND" represents all of the lands on the metaverse platform. MANA also serves as the foundation for native utility tokens used in transactional contexts.

We may anticipate plenty of investment possibilities in the Metaverse as we continue on our path to creating it.

The fundamentals of building a virtual world

It is essential to utilize the correct method and best practices while constructing a virtual reality world to improve the user experience. 'Design principles' is a term used in the concept of building a virtual environment. Design principles are a set of concepts or precepts that are universally accepted as true in projects of a comparable nature. These rules are different from conventional design in virtual reality.

Think about creating a two-dimensional design. It must have a design based on a grid or a visual hierarchy that is jam-packed with data and will direct people to the same crucial information. These guidelines and standards are developed over many years. It must go through a

125

great deal of testing and try and error. These rules may not always be followed, but there should always be a valid justification for doing so.

Since virtual reality is still a developing field, everyone participating in its construction is still learning the fundamental design principles. You should keep an eye out for things that don't work well in what you are making if you want to find the kind of design concepts that perform wonderfully well. As the virtual community continues to expand and consumer virtual reality applications increase, the best standards and practices will eventually become apparent. However, as of right now, there are still a few virtual reality standards in use, and you can use it on any platform. It makes no difference what you are designing.

Starting a virtual reality experience: some guidelines

A user will require some time to adjust to their new surroundings after they begin an encounter. To help people have a positive user experience, you should start your design with a straightforward open scenario where they can quickly integrate into it and exert wonderful influence over it. Don't just overwhelm it with a confusing open scenario that could take the consumer ten minutes to comprehend what is happening. Allow the player to take control of themself in the virtual setting and switch to the main game experience as needed. For instance, the game "job simulator" exists. You will land in a very tidy atmosphere when you first start this virtual game, and you can so far finish a simple assignment with the control you used to enter the game. The user will be able to relax, adapt to the surroundings, and even get used to the control they employ in the game by doing this.

directing the user's focus to the virtual reality environment

The next step in constructing a virtual environment is to draw users' attention to the virtual reality game. Comparing virtual reality to traditional 3D screens, the arrangement is quite linear. In virtual reality, you must allow the user the ability to look around and even explore their surroundings. Give them some time to get along with the surroundings. The only issue is that it might be difficult for you to draw their attention to a certain section of the application.

The user's vision must be framed by you, the Creator, so that it concentrates on what you want them to see. As a 3D content developer, you could find it challenging to decide how you want the user to interact with the main material that is concentrated on a certain area of the environment. And you are aware that you cannot force a user to look in a certain direction. In virtual reality, forcing the user to look in a particular way could make them queasy. There are numerous techniques for getting users to concentrate on the areas you want them to. You can utilize deceptive 3D audio cues to lead the user to the location of the action. Cues from lightning are another option. For instance, you might make the areas you want your user to focus on bright and the areas you don't want them to can be made dark to draw their attention. All of the app's content can also be reoriented to align with the user's direction.

Some virtual reality programs simply instruct the user to spin around and face wherever they want the player's attention by placing a message in their 3D surroundings. This method is also used in some games played in rooms. Users will only have a finite amount of available sensors to track their actual intentions in this case. It is very simple to be twisted around in room-scale virtual reality, but if you put up a message, it can help the user concentrate on the sensors in the actual world. The Robo Recall is a prime illustration of the room-scale virtual.

To manage the user's attention, you can employ any of the approaches outlined above. Whichever approach you use, it's vital to remember that virtual reality consumers may make their own decisions. You have the right to choose, but that right could conflict with what you want them to do. A well-designed virtual reality experience must find ways to provide the user freedom of choice while simultaneously focusing on them where you want them to be.

having complete grasp of the virtual reality comfort zone

The user interface cannot fill the entire canvas size with a standard 3D design. There is a size restriction on where the user interface may exist, though it is unclear whether this is due to the size of the monitor or the browser. This limitation does not apply to virtual reality. Before you discard the design, a 360-degree canvas is available. The user interface is accessible anywhere and everywhere. There are a few guidelines you should follow to ensure a comfortable experience before you start designing UI elements around your users. The virtual reality experience will be terrible and the user won't want to try your game again if they have to swivel their entire body, head, or eyes too much to see the text or fly about to use the user interface you built.

The eyes will strain to focus on items as they get close to the face; if the object is 0.5 meters away from the player, that is when straining is likely to begin. The distance between the things and the users should be 0.75 meters if you don't want the users to strain their eyes. When they are between 0.75 and 10 meters away, they can have a detailed perception of their surroundings. The strain effect will start to disappear at a distance of between 10 and 20 meters, and maybe after that.

Therefore, it is ideal to position your object between 0.75 and 10 meters away from the primary information that you want users to concentrate on. If the information is near up, it will strain the eye, and if it is far away, the intended impact won't be seen. Users should not stare upward more than 60 degrees, and they should not look downward more than 12 degrees.

Risk from metaverse potentials

Low reaction

Although the Metaverse appears to be the internet of the future, its viability is uncertain. The term "Metaverse," which Neal Stephenson used for his book "Snow Crash," described a virtual reality-based universe that replaced the internet. People in the scientific book employed several digital personas that represented their personalities to explore the online world. It served as a diversion from the harsh realities of their world. Mark Zuckerberg, the creator of Facebook, wants to create a metaverse thirty years from now. Even yet, it will be a means of escape for those who want to avoid the tough economics or the negative consequences of spending too much time in the Metaverse.

The user will spend time exploring the virtual environment, purchasing goods, meeting friends, and embarking on adventures with strangers. The metaverse is a network of various interconnected universes without any established rules. Although the Life metaverse promises to be great and worth the wait, it is uncertain whether many people will desire to travel the globe. Without having the guarantee that people will participate in the virtual world experience, they aim to create a world that is filled with a wide variety of fantastic things.

It might not be enduring

The Metaverse's capacity for persistence is one of its most important characteristics. The possibility exists that the Metaverse won't endure. It might not last as long as it has been predicted to. It's possible that the graphics will change over time. Due to the complex graphics, there may be an overload, which could cause the website or the computer used to view the Metaverse to crash. The crucial thing is that it might not persist indefinitely.

divisional level

Class division is another danger that can contribute to the Metaverse's demise. Some people will be left out of the latest trends because not everyone can afford to be on the Metaverse. Nobody enjoys missing out on activities that 80% of the world is engaged in. A significant rift between society's high and poorer classes could result from this. The equipment needed to explore the virtual world, such as headsets and other headgear, may be pricey. They'll probably be too pricey for the typical man to afford. The class divide will have an impact on society and could alter norms and beliefs that society may never fully recover from. The Metaverse should concentrate on preventing stratification of the economy. If there remains division, the world has not been brought together through the Metaverse.